FRIDAY 13

CHANG

Coca

TOP TEN

GW00869968

THAT'S AMAZING!

Strange Facts
with comments by
SPIKE MILLIGAN

illustrated by
Ann Slack of Hurlston Design

Ladybird Books

THAT'S AMAZING

I was born in India because I wanted to be near my mother. When my father saw me he wanted to be near his mother. My father wanted a girl. My mother wanted a boy so they were both disappointed.

I came from a very poor family, so poor I was born without any clothes on. When I grew older my father tried to get me into the army. They said, as I was only four, I was too young and could I come back when I was older. So my father waited until I was one hour older, but they said I was still too young. To avoid school I grew up very quickly. I went from four to sixteen in one year. I tried to join the Navy and they said, "Can you swim?" and I said, "Why, haven't you got any ships?" I made my living by drawing – every week I drew £27 social security.

Next I joined a rock group – we went around throwing rocks at people. As a result I got a job in a hospital as a patient with a split head. When I came out I tried to join the army again, as I was 83, but they said I was too old and could I come back earlier. So I died and lived happily ever after.

SPIKE MILLIGAN

Lord Nelson suffered from sea sickness.

His glass eye is coming up for auction – it's looking for a buyer.

An Italian miniature carver called Giovanni Rossi once carved 70 saints' heads in a cherry stone.

They gave him the pip.

After his execution Sir Walter Raleigh's head was embalmed and his widow carried it everywhere with her until she died 29 years later.

Elizabeth I (1533-1603) was extremely clean for her day – she took 4 baths a year.

ROYAL BATHTIME
SPRING ✓
SUMMER ✓
AUTUMN
WINTER

4

The most common family name in the world is Chang.

But you have to be Chinese. If you're English and your name is Chang - you are an imposter.

The Grimm brothers collected over 200 children's tales and legends. One aged soldier told his stories to them in exchange for old trousers.

In 1926 Rin Tin Tin, the Alsatian dog star, won an Oscar for Best Actor of the year.

5

On 7th December 1968 a man called Richard Dodd returned a library book taken out by his great-grandfather in 1823 from the University of Cincinnati Medical Library.

He's still paying the fine.

Johann Heinrich Karl Thieme dug 23,311 graves during his 50 year career as sexton at Aldenburg, Germany.

I don't dig that kind of work.

Mrs Gwen Mathewman of West Yorkshire knitted 885 garments in 1975, using 29,852 kg of wool, equivalent to the fleece of 85 sheep.

The Dottheimer flea lives and breeds only inside beermats in German pubs.

The earliest musical instrument known is the lyre. A picture of a lyre was found in an Egyptian tomb which was over 3,400 years old.

Attila the Hun was just 1 metre tall.

The tallest dwarf in the world.

The owl is the only creature which can turn its head in a full circle.

The coldest city in the world is Yakutsk, USSR, where the temperature can be as low as $-60°C$.

In 1890 Dennis Taverstock of Lancashire managed to compile a complete pack of playing cards from picking cards up in the street. It had taken him 31 years.

I'd never stoop so low!

A Russian woman, Eva Vassilet, gave birth to 16 pairs of twins, 7 sets of triplets and 4 sets of quads – 69 children altogether.

In the Middle Ages, hot oil was sometimes poured over castle ramparts to stop attackers scaling the walls. In Friesland on the North Sea, hot porridge was used instead, to stop marauding Vikings.

Why do middle aged people behave like this!

The most frequently sung song in the English language is "Happy Birthday to you". It was sung in space on 8th March 1969 by the *Apollo IX* astronauts.

A single sheep's fleece may contain up to 26 million fibres.

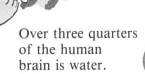

A married one is about the same.

In Lynn, Massachusetts, it is illegal to give coffee to children.

Over three quarters of the human brain is water.

When your nose starts to run, it means your brain is leaking.

In Egypt, if you can drive forwards and backwards just 6 metres you can pass your driving test.

Rhyming games have often led to the introduction of new names. One of the most famous was J M Barrie's Wendy in *Peter Pan*, from "fwendy-wendy".

Also Bed Pan from Potty Wotty.

The windiest place in the world is Commonwealth Bay, George V Coast, Antarctica, with several winds of 320 kilometres per hour each year.

Five piranha
and saddle

...an eat a horse
...in 5 minutes.

What's the hurry?

HIC!

A glass eye was fitted to a snake at London Zoo.

A Marsquake can last for an hour, while an Earthquake only lasts for seconds.

A Mars bar goes even quicker.

"Inbetweening" is a computer process used to work out the tiny changes necessary in each picture of a cartoon to make the characters "move".

I thought 'inbetweening' was what you put in sandwiches.

Edicoe Needles of Detroit, Michigan, used to eat an average of 75-100 pork chops a day.

Making a pig of himself!

At the age of 6 months Baby Leonard Meyer of Los Angeles had hair on his chest.

A sound takes a thousandth of a second to travel from one ear on your head to the other.

The initial wind velocity of a human sneeze is more than gale force 10.

In 1928 Henry Lewis, who played snooker with his nose, made a break of 46 points.

...ctoria's 9 children gave
... 64 grandchildren.

But she gave them back.

The firework Catherine Wheel is named after St Catherine who was tortured on a spiked wheel and then beheaded. She refused to marry the 4th century Emperor Maxentius.

After making the first solo expedition to the North Pole, Naomi Uemwa from Japan said he 'didn't like being alone'.

The number of computing elements in the human brain is about one hundred thousand million.

The computing elements in a computer are at best around a thousand million.

An average human brain has an intelligence rated at an IQ of about 100.

A computer's general intelligence is roughly that of a very stupid worm.

Captain Kidd, the pirate, was executed in London in 1701. He had to be hanged three times – the rope snapped twice.

But he only died once.

Henry VI was nine months old when he succeeded to the thrones of England and France in 1422.

An Italian, Count Meral, could part his hair without his fingers or a comb, by using only his scalp muscles.

Moses was cleverer, he could part the Red Sea.

A person's heart beats 40 million times in one year.

It takes 18 seconds for blood to return to the heart from the toes.

18 seconds

Blond beards grow faster than dark beards.

The longest recorded nose was 19 centimetres long and belonged to a Thomas Wedders.

If I had a choice, I'd never pick a nose like that.

A new baby breathes at the rate of about 40 breaths a minute, while a resting adult takes 13.17 breaths and as many as 80 when exercising strenuously.

TREMENDOUS JONES?

Babies born at sea were often named after the ship they were on at the time – Dolphin, Exeter, Pilgrim and Tremendous have all been examples.

I know a poor chap called Titanic.

18% of the fresh water flowing into the oceans of the world comes from the Amazon River.

The Ancient Greeks invented the yoyo.

Circus tights were invented in 1828 by bareback rider Nelson Hower when he appeared in his underwear because his costume hadn't been delivered.

'James' Barry was an officer in the British Army for 52 years from 1813 without anyone knowing 'he' was a woman.

It was a cover up.

Louis Cyr, a Canadian, could lift 247 kilograms with one finger.

The brain can remember more than 50,000 different smells.

A statue of Captain Hanson Gregory stands in Camden, Maine, USA. He invented the hole in the doughnut.

Until he patented it, he kept the hole locked in a safe.

The Empress Elizabeth (1345-1393), wife of German Emperor Charles IV, could rip a suit of steel armour from top to bottom with her bare hands.

Lin Ch'ung, a 15th century Chinese government official, was born with two pupils in each eye.

The first man to swim the English Channel was Matthew Webb. He crossed from Dover to France in 21 hours 45 minutes in 1875.

Webb feat.

Murder John Smith, born in 1878, was named after his father, Murder Smith.

In 1974 surfing clubs in Brisbane, Australia, found 250 sets of false teeth lost by bathers and surfers on Queensland's Gold Coast.

19

In 1907 a rainfall of 23.03 metres was recorded in the Khasi Hills, Africa.

All people only 23 metres tall, drowned.

The Australian tiger fish has enough venom in its sac to kill 30 sheep.

Judo was invented in the 1880s by Dr Kauo and derived from the old Japanese sport of ju-jitsu.

Henry VIII was a very keen wrestler.

The Olympic Games were played in honour of the ancient Greek god of gods – Zeus – at the foot of Mount Olympus.

Mount Olympus has feet?

Human hair used to be used to stuff tennis balls.

The first pocket computer – the Sharp P.C 1121 – was sold in 1980.

The human body contains enough phosphorus to cap the ends of 60 boxes of matches.

21

In the 19th century a dinner party was held inside a model of an Iguanodon – a dinosaur with spiky thumbs.

A tortoise takes four hours to travel 1.6 kilometres.

Lesson, don't travel on the M25.

G'Day

Dromedaries (camels with one hump) were first introduced into Australia in 1866 by explorer Robert O'Hara Burke. Now there are so many in central Australia that they are classified as vermin.

But they still look like camels.

The world's most popular vegetable is the onion.

Greenland is mostly covered by a thick sheet of ice. Eric the Red called it Greenland so that people would think it was a pleasant place to live.

He must have been thick as well.

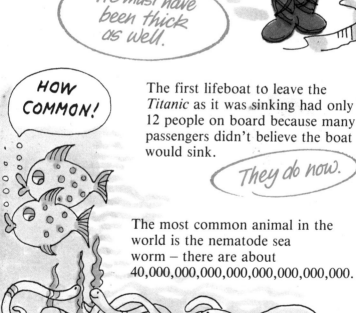

HOW COMMON!

The first lifeboat to leave the *Titanic* as it was sinking had only 12 people on board because many passengers didn't believe the boat would sink.

They do now.

The most common animal in the world is the nematode sea worm – there are about 40,000,000,000,000,000,000,000,000.

23

The Emir of Kuwait has an income of over one million pounds a day.

He only drinks milk, he's a milk sheik.

In 1975, the Rev Geoffrey Howard of Salford pushed a wheelbarrow across the Sahara Desert.

St Simeon Stylites lived on pillars – he stayed on one for an uninterrupted 37 years.

Richard the Lion Heart was King of England for 10 years, but only spent 6 months in the country.

Tax reasons.

Clinophobia is the fear of going to bed.

The best cure is to sleep standing up.

The most popular day in Britain for eating fish and chip shop meals is Friday.

Fry day?

A hurdy-gurdy is a mixture of violin, piano and barrel organ.

Handel wrote *The Messiah* in 24 days.

A zedonk is a donkey with striped legs – half zebra, half donkey.

If the stripes are at the front, it's called a donkzee.

If you're staying with someone in Denmark and they give you carrots to eat on your last day, it means they don't want you to come back again soon.

The door of Number 10 Downing Street can only be opened from the inside.

But the only way to get in is from the outside.

There is enough fat in an average man's body to make 75 candles.

Laika the dog was the first animal in space, launched by the Russians in *Sputnik 2* on 3rd November 1957.

The first landing on Mars of an unmanned probe was on 20th July 1976.

CRUMP

FRIDAY 13

Triskaidekaphobia is fear of the number 13 – many American hotels don't have a room or floor 13, but use the number 12b instead.

The Hawaiian alphabet only has 12 letters – a, e, h, i, k, l, m, n, o, p, u, w.

Lucky devils

Marie Antoinette drank only water.

She was up all night.

In the New York telephone directory are names such as Mona Lisa Gooseberry and Oscar Asparagus.

The skin is the largest single organ of the human body.

The other large organ is in the Albert Hall.

CRIPES!

Some earthworms in Western Australia are 2.1 metres long.

Dolphins sleep with one eye open.

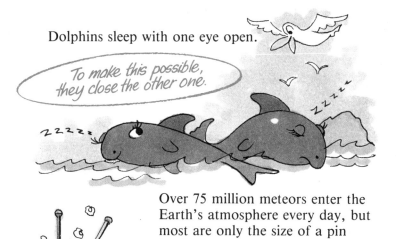

To make this possible, they close the other one.

Over 75 million meteors enter the Earth's atmosphere every day, but most are only the size of a pin head.

Until the 17th century, if princes were naughty, they weren't punished – but their 'whipping boy' was.

The first Woolworth store was opened in Utica, New York State, in 1879. Everything cost 5 cents.

A man can't have everything – where would he put it?

5 CENTS

5 cents

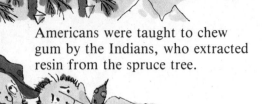

Americans were taught to chew gum by the Indians, who extracted resin from the spruce tree.

When Superman first appeared in Action Comics in 1938, he could not fly. He was, however, capable of leaping 190 metres, and running faster than an express train.

Did you know – Tokyo used to be called Edo? Chicago was called Fort Dearborn? Leningrad was called St Petersburg? And New York was New Amsterdam?

No, I didn't know.

Leonardo da Vinci took four years to paint the "Mona Lisa".

Elvis Presley had the highest number of hit albums – 90 altogether – and 35 in the top ten, but the Beatles had the most No. 1s – 12.

The first woman in space was Valentina Tereshkova in *Vostok 6* on 16th June 1973. At that time she completed 48 orbits of the Earth.

She was going round with three men at the same time.

Peking station's waiting room holds 14,000 people.

They're waiting for the train.

The world's smallest church is in Lanolia, Kentucky and has room for only three people.

The vicar stands outside and preaches through a keyhole.

On 27th November 1976 Doun Reynolds yodelled for 7 hours 29 minutes in Canada.

Twit!

A German military band played "God Save the King" at least 16 times on 9th February 1909 while King Edward VII attempted to put on the uniform of a German Field-Marshal in a train.

The German Field-Marshal was furious.

On 12th June 1979 Bryan Allen was the first person to cross the English Channel by a manpowered aircraft called *Gossamer Albatross*.

Every day of the year, 200 million people ask for a coke.

Which one of them gets it?

COKE PLEASE!

Growing dandelions in Pueblo, Colorado, is against the law.

When a man meets a cow in Pine Island, Minnesota, he is required by law to remove his hat.

It takes food from 12-36 hours to pass through the large intestine.

In Russia it takes that long to queue for it.

The longest railway bridge in the world is the Huey P Long Bridge in Louisiana, USA. It is 7 kilometres long.

It reached from one end to the other.

The largest number of people ever carried across the Atlantic in an airship was 117 – by the German *Hindenburg* in 1937.

A rat can smell X-rays.

I smell a rat.

Mrs Miriam Hargrave failed her 39th driving test when she crashed into a set of red traffic lights.

The earliest bicycle was built in 1839-40 by Kirkpatrick MacMillan of Dumfries in Scotland.

A record is a hit if it spends only one week at number 100.

On 8th November 1958, the *Melody Maker* published the first Top Ten album chart.

If four people are playing cards a player can expect a complete suit of cards once in every 39,688,347,497 deals.

Who can live that long?

Almost 500 years ago Leonardo da Vinci made the first technical drawings for a helicopter. The first helicopter that actually flew was produced by Igor Sikorsky at the beginning of World War II.

The first mechanical lift was invented in 1852 by Elisha G Otis in the United States.

But it only went up and down.

The guillotine – used in France for cutting off people's heads – was originally called the 'Louisette' after its inventor Antoine Louis. It was renamed after the doctor Joseph Guillotine who suggested that its use should be more widespread.

A small guillotine that only gave the criminals a nick was called a nicotine.

Garlic belongs to the Lily family.

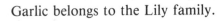

They must make a fortune.

In 1974 a farmer in England grew square tomatoes and apples.

On April Fools' Day, the New York Bronx Zoo got over 600 telephone calls for Mr and Mrs Wolfe.

The elephants had trunk calls.

Car number plates were introduced in Britain in 1903.

1A
22B

To make chips, silicon crystals that are 99.9999999% pure must be grown.

My Mother uses potatoes.

60% of a badger's diet consists of earthworms.

'Veteran' cars were manufactured before 31st December 1904.

'Vintage' cars are those made between 1st January 1917 and 31st December 1930.

It's very bad table manners in Germany to cut your potatoes with a knife – it should be done with the fork.

38

In May 1969, Paul G Tully of Brisbane ate 30 bags of potato crisps each weighing 56.6 grams in 24 minutes 33.6 seconds – all without a drink of any kind.

A man's jacket buttons from left to right so he can draw his sword easily.

Spike says, he unbuttons it to draw his pension.

In the USA each person eats about 48 ice creams a year. In the United Kingdom each person eats only 10.

Margarine was invented in 1869 by Hippolyte Mège-Mouriès.

Its popularity spread.

Napoleon Bonaparte was frightened of cats.

Had Wellington used cats instead of soldiers, the battle of Waterloo would have ended sooner.

Ten times more men than women are colour blind.

Humans walk approximately 104,608 kilometres in an average lifetime.

Roller skates were invented by Joseph Martin in 1760. It seems he skated into a London ballroom, playing a violin.

Mary Queen of Scots was a skilful billiards player.

Scientists estimate that 99% of the universe is made up of only two elements – hydrogen and helium.

The longest word in the Oxford dictionary is the 29-letter 'floccinaucinihilipilification'. It means worthless.

Not only means, but is!

'Karate' means empty hand – fighting without weapons.

CRACK!

41

Snow isn't white – it's transparent. It's the reflection of light off the crystals which makes it look white.

Snow isn't White and the seven dwarfs.

Pyjamas are worn in India during the day, but they are nightwear in Britain.

On the planet Venus the Sun rises in the west and sets in the east.

One teaspoon of water contains as many molecules as the Atlantic Ocean contains teaspoons of water.

How do they make teaspoons out of water?

The division of the world into time zones was introduced at the end of the 19th century. There are 24; each is approximately 15 degrees of longitude and represents 1 hour of time.

So when it's night-time in China, it's Wednesday over here!

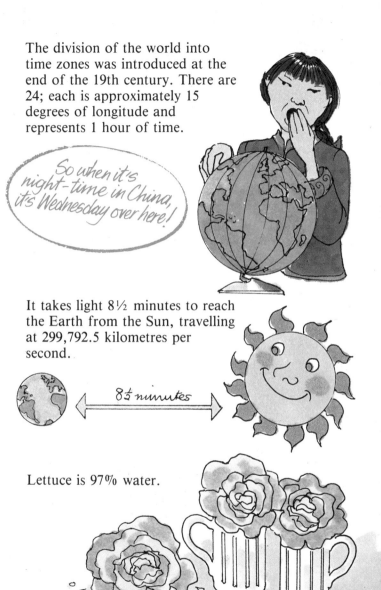

It takes light 8½ minutes to reach the Earth from the Sun, travelling at 299,792.5 kilometres per second.

8½ minutes

Lettuce is 97% water.